Echoes of Eckhart

In the teachings of the thirteenth-century mystic Meister Eckhart, Richard Skinner has discovered both welcome illumination for his own spiritual journey and the inspiration for these poems.

They do not simply replicate Eckhart's work, but offer glimpses behind the scenes – quirky speculations, which perhaps underlie his teaching, about encounters between Eckhart, creation, everyday life, and God.

Each poem stands on its own, and can be read by itself, but together they form a sequence in which Eckhart chops wood, confronts a pile of paperwork, receives a birthday present, plays hide-and-seek with God, dances in the desert – and goes to explore the wine cellar.

Richard Skinner, scientist by training, is a poet, workshop-leader and counsellor. He lives in Exeter, and has worked as a library assistant, psychiatric nurse, social worker and family therapist. His previous publications include the collections *Leaping & Staggering* and *Still Staggering …*, and the sequence *In the Stillness*, based on Julian of Norwich. He regularly gives readings of his work and – harking back to his time as a member of the Cambridge University Footlights – occasionally writes and performs sketch-based comedy.

RICHARD
SKINNER

Echoes
of
Eckhart

*An Utterance
Arising from the Works
of
Meister Eckhart*

CAIRNS PUBLICATIONS · SHEFFIELD
ARTHUR JAMES · BERKHAMSTED

First published in Great Britain by

CAIRNS PUBLICATIONS
47 Firth Park Avenue, Sheffield s5 6HF

in association with

ARTHUR JAMES LTD
70 Cross Oak Road, Berkhamsted, Herts HP4 3HZ

A catalogue record for this book is available
from the British Library

ISBN 0 85305 442 8

Typeset in Monotype Columbus by
Strathmore Publishing Services, London N7

Printed in Great Britain by
Guernsey Press, Ltd, Guernsey, C.I.

Contents

Introduction

I thought I had got away with it. While the others were offering to present various topics at future meetings, I had remained quiet and tried to look preoccupied. I didn't want the bother of having to prepare a discussion paper, and as one by one the dates were allocated to other group members it increasingly seemed that indeed the bother had passed me by ...

But ...

One date remained obstinately unfilled, and as the chairman turned to me I realised that my air of preoccupation was not going to save me after all. 'How about doing something on Eckhart?' he asked. 'Yeah, sure, fine, no problem,' I said, hoping that the gritting of teeth is a silent phenomenon.

So Eckhart it was for me, and with the date on which I had agreed to present a few ideas about him being many months in the future, I had plenty of time to panic about it.

This all took place at a meeting of a 'Green Group' of which I was a member. An initiative of Christopher Southgate, the above-mentioned chairman and at that time a pastoral assistant in the Chaplaincy at Exeter University, the group met roughly twice a term to explore the relationship between ecological issues and Christian theology. Eckhart had been referred to in passing at previous meetings, particularly in connection with the work of Matthew Fox[1], and as I had already expressed an interest in his thought not only at the group but also in private conversation with Chris, I suppose it was inevitable that I would be called on in this way. It turned out to be very fruitful to me that I was.

My interest in Eckhart had been kindled by Fox's *Meditations with Meister Eckhart*[2] and Cyprian Smith's *The Way of Paradox*[3] as well as having come across references to him in the works of the psychologist C. G. Jung[4] and in one or two books on mysticism[5]. I now began to read Eckhart himself, albeit in translation.

After presenting a brief, informal paper to the group I continued to read and re-read his work as an initially vague idea of writing a set of poems based on his thought became increasingly definite, principally as a way to focus and explore my own evolving beliefs. I started writing the poems at the beginning of

1995, quickly settled on the brief, gnomic approach, and discovered that Meister Eckhart insisted on appearing in person in every poem.

However, I should point out that the Meister Eckhart who chops wood, stares at the fire, dances in the desert and confronts a pile of paperwork in the following pages is not exactly the 13th/14th century figure of the same name, although the writings of the historical Eckhart gave birth (an appropriate Eckhartian term) in my imagination to the protagonist of the poems. The historical teacher, preacher, scholar and mystic is a powerful source of light, and a few rays emanating from him have been refracted through and coloured by my own experience and thinking to create the image of 'my' Meister Eckhart; and, of course, such an image is both similar to and different from the original. The poems therefore neither simply summarize the original Eckhart nor express a balanced view of his teachings. Anyway, 'balanced' isn't a word I'd associate with Eckhart, given his radical use of language.

Another factor to take into account is the existence both of 'scholarly' works in Latin and 'popular' works in the vernacular of Middle High German. Since, to give one example of the former, his exegesis of the first verse of the book of Genesis ('In the beginning God created heaven and earth') takes up what I would consider a mind-numbing eight pages, I am at the moment more than happy to leave in-depth exploration of his scholarly works to the trained theologian. His German sermons and treatises, though, are a different matter, with their startling images and powerful language conveying, in the words of Oliver Davies, 'Eckhart's desire to stir his audience, to waken them to new possibilities of spiritual vision.'[6] It is with a few rays of light from these works that the Meister Eckhart of the poems has been created.

Or, to change the metaphor, Meister Eckhart spoke, and what follows are echoes.

1 e. g. *Original Blessing* (Bear & Co., 1983)

2 Fox (1983a)

3 Smith (1987)

4 e. g. *Answer to Job* in *Collected Works, Vol. 11* (RKP, 1958)

5 e. g. Happold (1963) and Suzuki (1979)

6 Davies (1989)

Echoes

Fingerprints
Everywhere

Meister Eckhart examines them
Closely

The evidence is
Overwhelming

What could be fuller
Of the being of God
Than an angel?

Meister Eckhart is wondering

As there lands
On his lectern
A fly

A horse galloping
Around its meadow

Hello horse!
Says Meister Eckhart
What are you doing?

Enjoying myself
God laughs

A glorious day!
Meister Eckhart basks
In the sun

No matter how much
Heat
He absorbs

The sun
Continues
To shine

Dazzled
By the sun
Meister Eckhart can see
Only the sun

Later
Wherever he looks
Still he can see
Only the sun

A splendid tree!

Meister Eckhart is studying
Where trunk becomes
Branch

He stares and
He stares
But he can't see

The join

How deep
Are your roots?
Meister Eckhart wonders

How deep
Is the earth?
The tree rejoins

And what of
Your fruit?
Meister Eckhart enquires

In my fruit is
My origin
Replies the tree

Meister Eckhart tastes
The fruit
Pronounces it good

Two
Identical
Blades of grass

Meister Eckhart looks
More closely

Two
Different
Blades of grass

Every blade of grass
A different blade of grass

Meister Eckhart looks
More closely

Every blade
A blade

Of
Grass

Whenever Meister Eckhart
Steps
On a stone

He knows
He's stepped on a
Stone

Meister Eckhart quizzes
A stone he's stepped on

Such is his desire to know
God's every utterance

It speaks as well as
It is able

But God remains
Unspoken

Meister Eckhart brings to God
A stone

How shall I speak of you?
It asks

By being a stone
Says God

Pregnant?
With God!

A startled Meister Eckhart
Tries to wake up

Discovers
He's not asleep

Deep
In the Nothing

Beyond
All something

A birth

Whose?
Asks Meister Eckhart

Whose!
Comes the echo

Going deep
Into the ground
Of his soul

Meister Eckhart finds

God
Giving birth to
Himself

You want to see me?
Then look deep
Into your soul

Doing as he is told
Meister Eckhart looks deep
And deeper still

Nothing here!
He exclaims

Quite so!
Nothing answers

Bursting in on God
Meister Eckhart catches him
Naked
In his dressing-room

His garments of
Goodness and
Justice
Not enfolding him

Come in
Says God
And take me as
I am

Muscles bulge and
Bulge

God and Meister Eckhart
Are arm-wrestling

Neither can budge
The other

Call it a draw?
God offers

Meister Eckhart accepts
With relief

His humility is beginning
To flag

Now!
Cries God
Starting to pull

Meister Eckhart takes up
The strain and
Pulls

Between them
They stretch
Now

To eternity

Another year gone!
Another year older!
Meister Eckhart sighs

Not so! Not so!
I'm as young as ever!
His soul replies

Happy Birthday!
Says God
Hope you like the
Gift

Unwrapping it
Meister Eckhart finds
Eternity
In the present

Words!
Meister Eckhart frowns

Who's been writing
On my wax tablet?

A tablet already
Full of words

Is difficult
To write on

What *is* today?

Meister Eckhart pauses
Before writing the date

But of course!

Today is the first of
Eternity

Torrents
Are tipping down
As Meister Eckhart steps
Outside

Nothing better than
Standing in rain
For getting completely
Wet

Such rain!

With every drop that
Falls on the ocean
And becomes the ocean

The soul of Meister Eckhart
Falls into God

A game
Of hide-and-seek

God is
Cunningly concealed

Meister Eckhart is
At a loss

God deliberately
Clears his throat

What are you
Up to?
Meister Eckhart asks

Right now
Says God
I'm creating all creation

Meister Eckhart nods
And what of
Me?

You too
God retorts
You too

When did you
Start
Creating creation?

Meister Eckhart enquires

Now
Says God
And
Now and Now and Now and Now and Now

Creation
Is seeking entrance
To the soul of Meister Eckhart

No room!
No room!

His soul is
Already full

Down in the cellar
Of his soul
Meister Eckhart finds
The ground of God

Down in the ground
Of God
Meister Eckhart finds
The cellar of his soul

A barrel
In the cellar

In the barrel
Wine!

Meister Eckhart
Samples it

Ah!
True vintage!

In search of
Spilt lentils
Meister Eckhart scrabbles
On the floor

One
He finds stuck
In a crack between
Flag-stones

Regarding the lentil
As all his possessions
He instantly
Abandons it

Meister Eckhart is chopping
Logs

I could do that for you
God offers

You already are
Says Meister Eckhart

With one swing of
His axe
Meister Eckhart splits
A log

From deep within it
He has heard God
Cough

The axe slips
And strikes a stone

The spark which flashes out
Is darkness

Compared with the spark
In Meister Eckhart's soul

What
Are you doing?
God asks

I am doing what
I am doing
Says Meister Eckhart

Says God
How very
Wise

Hot work!

Meister Eckhart pauses
Wipes the sweat
From his forehead

The wall has been well-built
Breaking through is
Tough going

Allow me
Says God
Picking up

The sledge-hammer

Meister Eckhart sits
Contemplating
God

A beggar approaches
Contemplating
Soup

Meister Eckhart stops
Contemplating
God

A pan of soup comes
To the boil
Seethes up in a rush
Spills over the sides

Meister Eckhart cries out
For joy

He has seen
Another boiling
Another spilling over

Confronted by a
Pile of paperwork
Meister Eckhart groans

Where is God
When you need him?

Right here
Says a muffled voice
From the middle of the pile

In the middle of his fast
It arrives

Dear Meister Eckhart
Please come to our feast

Consternation!
Fast or feast?

No contest!

Meister Eckhart knows
How to enjoy himself

Sampling
The soup
Meister Eckhart grimaces

Oh for a sprinkling
Of divine
Love

Why life?

Meister Eckhart ponders
Deeply

For what
Purpose?

From the silence
A single
Word

And the
Word
Was

Yippee!

God and Meister Eckhart
Are doing the
Hokey-cokey

In out
In out
Together they sing

Meister Eckhart discovers
That's
What it's all about

How about
A prayer?
Meister Eckhart offers

Or fasting?
Or good works?
Or …

No, no!
God interrupts
What I really like is

Rest

Meister Eckhart looks
At God

God looks
At Meister Eckhart

Each looks
Through the same eye

How does Meister Eckhart
Meet
With God?

By meditation
And
Devotion?

By ecstasies
And
Grace?

Or by the fireside
And
In the stable?

Meister Eckhart gazes
At the grate

Where fire gives birth to fire
In the logs

Until the logs themselves
Are one with the fire

Meister Eckhart picks up
The poker

And pokes
The fire

Putting a log on the fire
Meister Eckhart marvels
As a flurry of sparks
Flies up

Each spark
Is of the fire
And the fire
Is in each spark

The spark in the soul
Of Meister Eckhart
Is not content

No creature
Can satisfy it
The whole of creation
Leaves it unfulfilled

Even God
Brings no repose

God
Has gone missing?

You
Wish to find him?

Then
You should seek him

Says
Meister Eckhart

Where
You last left him

What a signpost!

All its arms
Are blank!

All the ways
Unmarked!

Meister Eckhart steps out
With confidence

He will at least
Enjoy the journey

Footprints

Meister Eckhart follows them
Into the desert

Stones
And blades of grass
And silence

Something
Is standing in the way

Meister Eckhart examines it

The something looks
Suspiciously like

Himself

The day is hot
The journey long
Meister Eckhart can think of
Nothing but water

With every step
His thirst increases
His desire for water
Grows greater

At night he speaks
In eloquent terms
Of another thirst
A deeper desire

What the water-pipe
Is made from

Meister Eckhart
Cannot say

But the water
Tastes wonderful

Treading his path
Meister Eckhart sees
Other travellers treading
Other paths

Keep on travelling!
He calls out as
They wave to him and
He waves back

Meister Eckhart is leaning
On his stick

Along comes God
Who kicks

The stick

Away

Meister Eckhart sprawls
On the ground

His walking-stick
Broken in two

Where will he find
Another?

Another stick?
God offers

Helping Meister Eckhart
To his feet

It's guaranteed
Unbreakable!

Completely un-
Kick-away-able!

I give you my
Word

What
Are you seeking?
Asks God
Of Meister Eckhart

Nothing
He answers

Well done!
Cries God
You have already
Found it

Desert
God
And Meister Eckhart

How can he move on
With God
In the way?

Help rid me
Of God

Pleads
Meister Eckhart

God
Moves aside

Meister Eckhart
Moves on

A long
Journey

Past the limits
Of knowledge

Beyond the end
Of desire

Meister Eckhart
Tramps on

Enters
The darkness

Breaking through to the desert
Of not God
Meister Eckhart finds

Not wisdom
Not goodness
Not truth

But
The stillness of the God
Beyond God

The spark in the soul
Of Meister Eckhart
Penetrates to here

Here
The silent desert
That lies beyond God

Here
The simple stillness
Where no distinction peeps

Here
Where being is born
And life is conceived

And the spark in the soul
Of Meister Eckhart
Is content

In the silent
Desert
Meister Eckhart sees
A spark
Dancing

Taking off his
Shoes
He too begins
To dance

The spark in the soul
Of which he
Insistingly speaks

Has become
In Meister Eckhart
A fire

Raging with life

Leaving God behind
In the silent desert

Meister Eckhart enters
The noise of the market

But God
Has beaten him to it

A church
Empty?

Meister Eckhart strides
Undeterred
To the lectern

Preaches to the poor-box
Impassions the pews

What's this?
A cloak stuffed under a pew?

Someone has been praying
And left it there

Inside the cloak
Meister Eckhart finds

God
Suffocating

Words echo
In the soul of Meister Eckhart

He utters them

The words go forth
The words remain within

Who needs
All these words
When you could have God?

So saying
Meister Eckhart sits down
And shuts up

Meister Eckhart:
His Life
&
Chronology
&
Selected Bibliography

Meister Eckhart: His Life

Meister Eckhart, whose Christian name is unknown
but traditionally said to be Johannes, was born *c.* 1260
near Erfurt in the province of Thuringia, in eastern
Germany. He probably received his education in Paris
among other places, and after a spell as both Prior of
the Dominican house at Erfurt and Vicar of Thuringia,
and having had the distinction, shared only with
Thomas Aquinas, of twice holding the Chair in
Theology at the University of Paris, he was appointed
Vicar-General at Strasbourg. Here his duties included
the spiritual and pastoral oversight of the many
women's religious communities and convents in the
region. A popular and seemingly tireless preacher,
many of his sermons were transcribed by members of
his congregations, and these sermons, along with two
or three other works also in the vernacular tongue of
Middle High German, complement his more formal,
academic writings in Latin.

Some of his views, expressed in an audacious and
often startlingly paradoxical style, eventually brought

him into conflict with the church authorities, who accused him, among other things, of promulgating pantheism. One examination in 1325 into the orthodoxy of his teachings exonerated him from the charge of heresy, but a second investigation a year later resulted in a number of his utterances being condemned as heretical (although church politics rather than theology may well have played the dominant role in the process that resulted in his condemnation). However, Eckhart did not live to know of the verdict, dying, it is believed, several months before the Papal Bull was issued in 1329.

His work was suppressed, but his influence could not so easily be eradicated, and his teachings maintained a kind of subterranean existence for centuries before re-emerging in the middle of the 19th century, when a German edition of a number of his writings was published. His popularity has continued to grow since then, with both his verbal daring and his actual teaching – and the two cannot be separated – exerting a powerful fascination and proving as fresh and invigorating as they did when he was alive.

Meister Eckhart: A Chronology

c. 1260 Born in Thuringia

c. 1275 Joins the Dominican Order, probably at the
        local priory in Erfurt. Starts a training in the
        Arts (grammar, logic & rhetoric) possibly in
        Paris

1293 To Paris, as a Reader, studying Peter
        Lombard's *Sentences*

c. 1295 Prior of Dominican convent in Erfurt and
        Vicar of Thuringia

1302 Receives his degree from the University of
        Paris and thereafter is known as Meister;
        appointed to one of the two chairs in
        Theology

1303 Provincial of Saxonia – administrative and
        diplomatic duties entailing much travelling

1311 Returns to Paris to chair of Theology.
        Duties involve writing a commentary on the
        scriptures

1313	Vicar-General of the Dominican province of Teutonia
c. 1323	To Cologne, with pastoral and academic duties
1325	Nicholas of Strasbourg conducts a critical examination into his work, leading to an exoneration of suspicions of heresy
1326	Henry of Virenberg initiates inquisitorial proceedings against him
1328/9	Dies
1329	A Papal Bull is issued condemning 15 articles as being heretical

A Selected Bibliography

Translations

Clark, J. M., and Skinner, J. V., *Treatises and Sermons of Meister Eckhart* (Harper & Row, 1959)

Colledge, E., and McGinn, B., *Meister Eckhart: the Essential Sermons, Commentaries and Defence* (Paulist Press, 1981)

Davies, O., *Meister Eckhart: Selected Writings* (Penguin, 1994)

Fox, M., *Breakthrough* (Doubleday, 1980)

Fox, M., *Meditations with Meister Eckhart* (Bear & Co, 1983a)

Walshe, M. O'C., *Meister Eckhart: German Sermons & Treatises,* 3 vols (Element Books, 1987)

Books about Eckhart

Davies, O., *Meister Eckhart: Mystical Theologian* (SPCK, 1991)

Forman, R. K. C., *Meister Eckhart: The Mystic as Theologian* (Element, 1991)

Smith, C., *The Way of Paradox* (DLT, 1987)

Other books

Davies, O., *God Within* (DLT, 1988)

Davies, O., *The Rhineland Mystics* (SPCK, 1989)

Fox, M., *Original Blessing* (Bear & Co, 1983)

Happold, F. C., *Mysticism: a study and an anthology* (Penguin, 1963)

Suzuki, D. T., *Mysticism Christian and Buddhist* (Unwin Paperbacks, 1979)

Far fuller bibliographies can be found in, e.g., Davies, 1994.